Disaster Tourism

Disaster Tourism

Poems

Rena J. Mosteirin

AMERICAN POETS CONTINUUM SERIES NO. 217

BOA EDITIONS, LTD. ◎ ROCHESTER, NY ◎ 2025

Manufactured in the United States of America

First Edition
23 24 25 26 7 6 5 4 3 2 1

Publications by BOA Editions, Ltd.—a nonprofit corporation under section 501 (c) (3) of the United States Internal Revenue Code—are made possible with funds from a variety of sources, including public funds from the Literature Program of the National Endowment for the Arts; the New York State Council on the Arts, a state agency; and the County of Monroe, NY. Private funding sources include the Max and Marian Farash Charitable Foundation; the Mary S. Mulligan Charitable Trust; the Rochester Area Community Foundation; the Ames Amzalak Memorial Trust in memory of Henry Ames, Semon Amzalak, and Dan Amzalak; and contributions from many individuals nationwide. See Colophon on page 137 for special individual acknowledgments. Any use of this publication to "train" generative artificial intelligence (AI) technologies to generate text is expressly prohibited.

Cover Art: "The Spirit of the Sea" by Roslyn Rose
Cover Design: Sandy Knight
Interior Design and Composition: Isabella Madeira
BOA Logo: Mirko

BOA Editions books are available electronically through BookShare, an online distributor offering Large-Print, Braille, Multimedia Audio Book, and Dyslexic formats, as well as through e-readers that feature text to speech capabilities.

Cataloging-in-Publication Data is available from the Library of Congress.

BOA Editions, Ltd.
250 North Goodman Street, Suite 306
Rochester, NY 14607
www.boaeditions.org
A. Poulin, Jr., Founder (1938-1996)

Contents

Part One: An Alarm

Part Two: No Home

Part Three: The Encrypted Latina

Part One: An Alarm

An Alarm

is going off and I'm being told
to ignore it. Put your fingers in your ears.
It will stop eventually. In some apartments
there is always that terrible noise:
the smoke alarm screwed in by the landlord
last year, now that the cheap batteries are dead
it chirps at a broken tempo.
People say if you grow up
with this bright screech in your ears
it hurts you less to hear it now. They are liars.
Listen to the dog whose vocal cords have been cut
and she spends her days trying to bark anyway.
No batteries will let her howl.
This is how power works in the world:
I once saw two police officers shoot a Hawaiian woman dead
through the windshield of a stolen car.
No alarm went off for her
and that's when I realized
my own vocal cords were cut.
I could not scream
and battery acid flooded my useless throat.
Now there is always a ringing bell
for her in the part of my heart I ignore.

Her Name

They said it on the news that night
and it chattered out of my head immediately.

We sat on the couch waiting for the television
to confirm what we saw. The teeth of the couch

were chattering off the hook. The news
was a horrible joke. It was 2004. We didn't have

cell phones or Internet—there was no immediate
way to see the news, we had to hold onto each other

chattering our teeth off the edge of the couch.
The couch had serious substance abuse issues.

The couch wanted to eat us alive. The couch
wanted to shoot us twice through the windshield of the car.

On the news they talked about a high-speed chase.
Yes. We'd seen that part. Here it is!

There was no cell phone footage
of the police actually shooting her.

There was no reporting of it.
Her name was given, and the fact that she died,

but the news made it seem
like it had something to do with stealing

a car, with driving too fast. There was no outrage.
There was no proof of the police shooting her.

Nothing but what we had seen and we were twenty years old
and jobless and drop-outs and the couch

was seriously trying to kill us and maybe
we didn't see what we thought we saw.

We didn't own cell phones. We ran away.
Those dreary afternoons after the shooting,

I went to the beach across the street
during the mist-time when the sea turns white

and there is no line between air and ocean
and there is no death. What I mean is, after dying

the ocean breathes itself back into you. No.
The mist is your after-death breath

and the ocean is your new body. No. That's not it.
There was no outrage because she was brown.

Native Hawaiian. What if the cops shot a tourist?
What if the cops shot us? That's why we ran away.

Why can't I remember her name?
Was it Rena? No. That's my name.

Hysteria

I screamed a stripe in my throat.
I stopped breathing
and turned blue. My eyes

were stars, then skies. I didn't
recognize my family, then
my own face in the mirror.

Never mind that—this is not
about my family. I don't
really need a family. The light

filled up my eyes until
I turned dark. I couldn't tell
if there were other people

in the room. I started to shout.
The sun flickered and went out.

Murdered Woman

Eyes gloaming, she/ parted the grass faithfully
in the evenings/ and found a different door
every time./ So she thawed the doors down
and glazed the mud/ supported the head, sculpted
an intelligent forehead/ and a wide, flat roof
for dancing/ on the top of the city/ eyes closed, arms out
to the wind/ full of color/ all the colors the day made.
The sun rises/ like Lazarus/ she inherits death
in the morning/ learns history/ makes decisions/ so many separate
traumas/ they are all doors. Doors or birds.
Her face feels colors as wing\bird/wing
blending cheek, chin, neck, forehead and feathers. Feathers
carving heads from mahogany and bodies/ feathers beating codes
into keypads/ making triangular doors open
behind her eye-ing eyes/ one by one/ in clear, bright color/
fluid/ wrapped in sweetgrass/ using phrenology to misunderstand/
proportions. Hang this/ on the walls in the rooms where war
is declared and denied, hang/ this, in a frame
is the face/ of the trauma/ she inherited
the porcine sky and/ naked mountaintops of the mind/
she refuses any knowledge of or association with history.
She doesn't need the dead to relive their deaths for her.
Her head is shaped to see the city as country.
(Translation: Her country-head is city-shaped so as to see.)

Rave

You woke up in the back of a van
certain you had been kidnapped.
There was a strange man who told you to relax.
All you could remember from the night before
was one red plastic cup
and stepping on the broken tops of burnt sugarcane.

Last night there was a rave
but your memory is covered over with red plastic. You don't have
a single song left, not one dance. Just a dose
and your mind snapped shut.

You pulled the handle and it opened
and you were out of the van and away from that man
and you tripped over the burnt torsos of broken sugarcane
now all flattened from dancing the night before
but you didn't have a night before. You woke up in his backpack.
You woke up in his back pocket.

You are free. You are free to go. You pull
the handle and let yourself out. He is still talking.
You can't hear him anymore. Forget that this happened,
forget the broken topazes of burnt sugarcane.
Don't even think roofies, rape, rave. Don't even think it.
You haven't been kidnapped, that's joy.

You can't see last night in your memory anyway,
so just keep letting yourself out of the van. Feel the joy
of an unlocked door. You have not been kidnapped.
You are free. You are free. You are free.

Disaster Tourism

Florida is a great place to lie.
The sun never sets. We don't have funerals.
You only ever know your friend passed
when you see his furniture at
the second hand store. You tell people,
I think he went back to Boston.
He wanted to be closer to the grandkids.

I accidentally found the place on the beach
where the attractive young people are.
I don't fit. These things are not democratic.
Beauty is basically fascism, in that
it's all about control. You can spoil yourself
so easily if you lose your grip.

This is how I will remember Naples, Florida
the Christmas after the hurricane.
The fishdock is a line of broken teeth.
The water is not safe for swimming.
Storm debris shimmers like souvenirs.
The red tide is a Christmas thing, he says.

The house is split and half slants down.
Just a few inches. Enough to show
that the foundation is unstable.

The ocean pushed up the concrete here.
You see that? It seemed so permanent.
This one is gutted. Oldest house on the beach.
Sold for the land on the condition that the new owner
tear down this dump. It's been condemned by the city.

When the water came, we swam.
Dolphins shopped on 5th Avenue.
All the storefronts are just facades.
This is where we go to play at being rich.

Tell me the part that's going to be the most expensive to fix.

Knoxville

I'd like to thank the painters of the Renaissance,
said the Mexican teenager at hip-hop night
at a bar in Knoxville where everyone was white

and earlier that day, a woman named Heather
was killed while counter-protesting in Virginia;
white supremacists killed her. I looked around

the room at this bar I'd never seen, in this city
I'd never set foot in before, and the poetry was bad, sure,
but what if this was some white supremacist

shindig and I'd stumbled in? Oh Tennessee, is today
the day I punch a Nazi? The Mexican teenager finished
reading his poem and the tattooed, tight-jeaned, short-haired,

white people of Knoxville, Tennessee stood up and cheered.
I was wrong to fear them but not wrong to fear.

Dixie

Your first night in Dixie, your blind date
                                                            says he started hallucinating
after the first twenty stabs, that's
                                                            when he realized nobody at the party
had his back, and death was flashing
                                                            like a light in the corner of one eye,
each time the knife went in, the light would blink
                                                            and everything that was not the light
swam farther and farther away.

Atlantic City

We paid extra for our big table, front, left—
just off the stage—the bride-to-be and her girls.
We paid for these attractive men to flatter us. In exchange,
we scream too loud. We lip weak drinks. I understood
that the men would take their clothes off. I wasn't expecting the
backstories. This guy did eight tours in Afghanistan,
the off-stage voice announces, and I see it—
he killed too many people. They surround him, still.
Dancing, the men come closer, their pain gets brighter
and everyone is screaming, not just the ghosts. Too loud, I leave
with Devika. She just got back from India. We walk
into the middle of the night in Atlantic City, New Jersey.
Cars keep pulling up next to us, the men inside
whistle and laugh, turn down the music, beg us to get in.
When I was living in Calcutta, Devika says, I walked
over dead bodies every day. You can get used to anything.

The Emperor of Ice-Cream

Pajama Pants sat in the hallway
of the mental hospital playing air guitar
as if he were sitting on the street
where people passing might leave some change.

My father called this the bum buck
and he always had one for the ice-cream truck
so the no-money kids could get something cold and sweet.
Give and receive, it's the same gesture, he said.

When I checked myself in, Pajama Pants sat in the hallway.
He didn't look homeless, with that shaved-smooth face.
Picked clean by heroin, he looked like a younger
version of my father, who was always playing guitar.

My father loved the no-money kids,
so I picked up an imaginary guitar
and I sat on the floor next to Pajama Pants. I said,
Hey man, would you teach me how to play?

The Cardboard People Have Their Own Rules

Proust gave his aunt's old couch to prostitutes
and then he found he couldn't visit them anymore
because seeing them sitting on his aunt's couch
brought him back to his childhood.

Some people are so big and beautiful
it seems that they are made of cardboard.
The cardboard people have their own rules.
Familiarity is a kind of blindness.

A good couch is as essential for a house
of prostitution as it is for an asthmatic nostalgist.
Proust felt bad for the couch,
how much it had come down in life.

They paid for the couch by telling him
things that didn't make sense.
Summer is the big-hearted season,
the bleeding breast of the year; the suicides
of August show that the world ends in summer smother;
it's always already not enough. All the maps
smell like church, I mean, holy water and mold.

Now I add my voice, my moment: Look Marcel, the
libraries are filling up with algorithms of love.

You Are So Beautiful

Our first night in London we got locked in Regent's Park. The park closes at dusk but no one told us. Dusk in the park is so nice—the sky gets all pink—we watched a group of teenagers climb a locked gate, still sure we could find an open exit. At each gate there is a map of the park, and I pulled out my cell phone and pointed it at the map and looked for the next exit and we went to it. Locked. Locked. Locked. A stranger on the street urged us to climb over. There's no way out, he said.

The next day at brunch in the West End we got that perfect outside table: a little fenced-in corner of the sidewalk just for us. Homeless men came by and pressed themselves to the gate and told us jokes and begged and gave us compliments and begged and one young man just held the bars in his shaking hands.

I hid my designer bag. I gave the beggars nothing. We ate half the food we ordered. We threw every other word away.

Big Ariana

At the National Portrait Gallery in London a man introduces himself as God to the security guard. Then we leave for Bond Street, where the shops are closed but there is a little grey mouse with peach pastel ears running between racks of flower-colored dresses. He belongs here. He matches.

When we reach Soho's secret tearoom the bartender makes a phone call and then we are allowed behind the bar and up the stairs where the walls are painted mouse-ear color and all the drinks taste faintly of roses. I sketch my husband while he looks at the map. He points out that one spot in Fitzrovia where the streets are busy changing their names.

Right at that moment, in Manchester, a man explodes himself at an Ariana Grande concert. Ariana Grande means Big Ariana. Twenty-two teenage girls are killed. Terrorism. Extra police float the streets with machine guns. I pretend they are balloons. Vividly I paint them with primary colors.

Defensive barrage balloons hovered over this city during World War II, I saw them sketched in charcoal at the British Museum. I pretend the occasion for all these police is a royal wedding, not the death of so many dancing teenage girls.

A perfume maker's shop features hot air balloon decorations. Grateful Londoners associate balloons with protection. I am afraid of the police. One department store is open later than the rest, a little girl in a pink dress presses herself to the glass of the window and stands perfectly still.

Half the Bitches in this Place Were Hanged for Treason

at the National Portrait Gallery, London

When Anne Boleyn laughs, her necklace with the large letter "B" shakes the three drop-pearls hanging from it and they clack together. B is for Baller, that's what she tells everyone, but Catherine of Aragon (Henry's first wife), likes to say B is for Beheaded. Elizabeth I hides her wings under pearls and a thick coat of white marzipan. Anne of Denmark hides her wings lower, under her hip-ruffles. She wears braided ropes of pearls so white they are almost black. Slung across her chest like that they are almost bullets. If they were oblong, she could be a commando, her machine gun amply supplied. Flora MacDonald holds a letter on her lap sealed with red wax as the bloodstained sun goes down behind her. In the boat four men are rowing with two at the helm—Flora and the man she went to jail for. Queen Caroline gave birth to seven surviving angels. Each are painted deliciously, in clotted cream and rose tones. Elizabeth, Queen of Bohemia, is bored. To her right Ben Johnson begs with his eyes. "You must have me confused with Anne from Denmark," she says, "that bitch over there, far end of the wall. The one with the face like a sheep." Henrietta Maria pawned her jewels for weapons during the Civil War but in her portrait she's got a crown, earrings, a necklace, a jeweled fan and a dress with pearls sewn into the fabric. The sleeves and the hem are heavy with the weight of all those weapons. Her baby, King Charles II, has a fancy little puppy in his lap and holds a jeweled dagger—red at the tip. He wears it around his neck on a chain of black and gold. He is taught that when the jewels run out, the fork at the table can be a weapon, and of course, there are always fingernails. Queen Anne was pregnant eighteen times but none of her children lived beyond eleven years and so ended the Stuart line. Mary, Queen of Scots, wears her Catholic cross on a choke chain. She is giving everyone the stink-eye. At night she cracks dead baby jokes and Queen Anne pretends not to hear them, but Anne Boleyn laughs her ass off.

Arms & Legs

after the murals of José Clemente Orozco, Baker Library, Dartmouth College

Give the children arms covered in feathers, ending in talons. Give the children armfuls of wheat. Fire arms. Water arms. The arms of the vultures are wings. Fist arms. Axe arms. Stabbing arms. Stealing arms. A straight arm draped in robes. The crooked arms of a dictator. The small arms of schoolchildren, walking. Sword as arm. Piston-pump arm. Arms pulling levers. Two arms digging. Arms that shovel. Arms that shield. Starved-thin arms. Muscular arms. A kiss on the elbow. A worker propped up on his arm, reading a book. An arm carved into an arm. A fist to the sky, where a snake turns into an arm. A kiss for your arm.

Lunging legs. Legs of white bone. Legs at rest. Legs twisted around each other. Legs tucked into the volcano. Legs frozen into claws. Legs under robes. Legs braced against the turning wheel. Flash of thigh with the skin pulled back, tendons straining and holes through the feet. White tights covering white legs. Legs bare down to schoolgirl socks, ending in tight black shoes. Pitched forward in labor legs. Bare shins boned down to broad feet. Legs turning into roots. Legs encased in metal. Wheel-spoke legs. Hammering legs. Scaffolding legs. Legs pegged into the totem pole. Buddha sits on crossed legs. The painter took his tools and went for the legs, again and again. Naked bodies, belly-forward, pushed on by the legs of Gods. The legs of the skeletons are just sticks, they don't mean anything. Snakes twine up and around the legs. Snakes turn into legs. The schoolteacher drills down her legs. Columns are the legs of the buildings. A leg turns into an ocean wave. Here, hold his legs, while we carve out his heart.

The Lady with the Unicorn

after a series of tapestries in the Musée de Cluny, Paris

Bring in the smallest animals, the weavers. I'm hoping for something gold to make her shine. She splits the forks and flies away in the wind, two hungry tongues. Lion, you must always know your hunter. If you can't take your eyes off him, you are too close to the art. Please step back. Singing music to them will make your servants grow louder. Please step back as her flag splits and bends. You are too close to the art. Your young men take flowers and join history because they feel obligated to the future, to the national culture. Here at the top, you are too close to the art. Please step back. The heron in the tapestry stands on one leg and watches us. She is a chain/ wearing my chain/ she laughs. I made a tapestry with her. Unicorns are loyal as lions are hungry. The unicorn keeps her mouth shut. A shut cell where prisoners were kept. A man who tried to be forgotten.

Bright Blue

I left for college that morning.
The bright blue mushroom trip
the night before was a chemical way
to say goodbye to my high school
best friend. I was still tripping
a little bit when the first tower
was hit. I was in a rented car
with my parents. All my
belongings were with me, college-bound.
It was a bright blue morning
when the traffic stopped. My parents
were praying and playing the radio.
Turning off the news and playing Beatles songs
and then turning that off to pray and then
playing news radio and then turning
it off to pray. On the radio they said
it was an accident, at first. Pray.
A plane flying into a building. News.
Everyone knows how dangerous
those small planes can be. Then
it was another plane, no accident.
Fuzzy grey reports were coming
from Washington, D.C.
We didn't have phones
and we couldn't check the news.
I mean, the news was on the radio
and the radio seemed confused.
Praying was also confusing.
Who were we praying for?
Ourselves? Were we in danger?
I didn't feel scared, I felt
vaguely and obscurely guilty.
A side effect? A holdover from the
mushroom trip? I felt,
in a way I couldn't exactly name,

that I was responsible for what
was happening to the city.
When the traffic started to move again
I fell asleep in the back seat,
leaning on a black trash bag full of clothes.
I hadn't slept the night before.
I did not own a suitcase.
When I woke we were in Connecticut
and the sky was bright blue again
and if we avoided turning on
the radio, we could pretend
nothing was wrong.

No Sweden

You were busy catching clouds in cheesecloth
and squeezing out the milk. In Sweden

there are berries called cloudberries.
In America we have no cloudberries

and if you are raped, the police will ask what were you wearing
and no matter what you answer, they will not believe you.

No witness, no evidence, no Sweden
inside the body. But a little basket

of strawberries are sitting next to the door
to your apartment when you get home. I put them there.

I can hear you crying through the bathroom wall.

Dear Rena

In Paris, I watched the sun rise and rise
over the river, across the bridges, and shine
through the top of a tugboat
made of glass and lit up like a lighthouse.

In Paris, the architecture has strong shoulders and a firm chin.
In Paris, I wrote to you
but I dropped the letter on the ground,
and the words fell off the page and turned into breadcrumbs.
Words can do that, right?
Pigeons pecked them up.

Paris put words into my hands.
Everywhere I went, I was eating bread and other nouns.
In Paris, I was made of pink marble.

In Paris, the dead met me
on the bridge, but I don't speak French,
so we stayed silent.

When the air is stale in Paris, it rains.
When it rains in Paris, everything
blooms into gray stone sculpture.

In Paris, I pushed my nails into the palms of my hands.
In Paris, I ignored your texts.
In Paris, I clawed at ledges.

In Paris, there is an island
in the middle of the river
where the famous church
still stands, burned out but not abandoned.

During the day they're rebuilding,
but in this famous church, at night, it's just the rats.
Remember when we snuck in
so you could play music
off a small speaker connected to your phone?

In Paris, we danced. Your music
made the church rats run away.
In Paris, we got arrested.
In Paris, we ate snails.
In Paris, we danced like church rats.

Part Two: No Home

Empathy Cut with Fentanyl

I'm in the emergency room.
It's winter and I'm in the emergency room again
this time it's my husband
when he fell his neck kissed the corner of the desk,
shoulder cracked on the way down and he curled up
crying into the floor. Couldn't move, wouldn't let me touch him,
I should have called an ambulance,
but I'm afraid to dial 9-1-1.

I'm in the emergency room.
It's winter and I'm in the emergency room again
and when my husband is wheeled out for scans,
a man comes in who was stabbed.
He is by himself and the nurse asks
if he's got anyone at home and he says no
and he asks for Fentanyl—
that's the moment the nurse turns on him,
decides the man stabbed himself.
Soon the cops will come.

I want to step in, before they hurt him.
He doesn't have anyone at home.
Does he have a home?
Even if my husband is not ok now, he will be ok
because I will take care of him.
I can take care of them both.

No, I can't. This man is a stranger.
I'm in the emergency room, where it is always winter.
When the cops come how will the nurse tell them?
Maybe lead with the loneliness diagnosis—
he doesn't have anyone at home. Does he have a home?

The least I can do is sing to him, quietly. He looks at me.
Nods along. Smiles. *Hey, you've got to hide your love away...*

Blindfold

Five years is the average
life expectancy after you start
sleeping on the street.
Homelessness, sleeping rough,
maybe sometimes you need
to integrate with the weather,
my mother tells me. On average
you will live for five years
since the first night of rough sleep. Good thing
you'll only struggle for five years
like that, she says. My mother
teaches me how to see the little white
square of light that follows you
wherever you go. When you die,
that square will open up, she tells me.
That square will become a door
and Jesus will give you a blindfold
so all that heaven-light
doesn't scorch your retina
which is the part of the eye
hurt by too much love.

Queens, New York

At the church my mother drops the host
and the priest refuses to give her another one.
She did it on purpose, he snarls.
She dropped the body of Christ.

When my mother taught Sunday school
the kids drew vampires, misunderstanding
everything she said about Jesus
coming back from the dead.

Hi, I'm Vladimir, a man at the wedding
says to my mother. Like Vladimir Putin.
I'm Adolf, she says, because this is
how she flirts. Like Adolf Hitler.

If you are in danger, you should run,
says the illuminated sign in the train station.
Is the vodka sweet or sour? The wedding DJ
sings out the question. Every table has a bottle.

If you are in danger and you can't run,
you should hide. We were hardworking peasants,
my mother says, looking at Vladimir.
No one is talking about Ukraine.

If you are in danger and you can't run
and you can't hide, you must fight.
The vodka is sour. How did I wind up here?
Vladimir, won't you ask Adolf to dance?

Skunk Hour

I was in an East German prison, when you said, Easter smells like white vinegar. That was nice, as if coloring eggs was a thing they did to lift the spirits of prisoners behind the Iron Curtain. Why was it 1988 in my dream? In 1988 I was five years old. But last night I was thirty-five and the Berlin Wall had been rebuilt. Honestly, it was a welcome departure from my Cuban prison dreams. You get it, right? All Cold War kids inherit this dull-colored fear.

Omi taught me how: yellow from onionskins, red from beet peels, and what did we use to make blue? You put a bowl of white vinegar next to our bed while we slept, to cut the harsh skunk smell that blew in the window. In my dream we figured out a way to make all the eggs inky blue—we used pens—and when we ate the eggs, our teeth turned black and fell out. Then I woke up, sick off the smell of vinegar and skunk spray.

We are at war with the skunks. Tonight they have won. This is how you trap a skunk:

1. Bait your mid-sized cage.
2. Stay close with a large, black towel.
3. When the skunk is in, cover the trap with the towel.
4. Lift the covered cage into the backseat of your car.
5. Drive that skunk as far away as you can.

& what do we use to make blue? Ink from pens, but what else? Deepest blue comes from driving as far away as we can. In 1989 the teeth fell out of the Berlin Wall and somehow my parents got hold of a chunk and we put it on top of our piano. The songs we would sing to it were wall-colored, but the great works of German composers always came out like Easter eggs: onionskin-yellow, beetroot-red and the blue-black of dead teeth.

Line of Ash

You drink
too much,
pass out
on a heap
of your
own
dirty
laundry,
burning
cigarette
in hand.

You wake
to a line
of ash
held
through
the night,
cigarette
hold-
ing
her shape,
hold-
ing
a vigil.
At stake:
skin,
hair,
bones,
teeth,
fabric,
all.

You
are
alive
clutch-
ing
what
is
left.

It is not until you see the neighbor's barn burn—it takes that blue blaze—to make you realize the absolute weight of it, to make you understand that suicide would have been the watchword.

Barnfire

Dreaming, the fire sounded
like *kish* and *tick*. Narrow sounds.
I woke to the open window,
to the barn on fire. I woke you.
Then I stood in the kitchen blankly
while you ran out into the night
wearing only your underwear.

The miscarriage ghosted my vision
a narrow pain burned up and through,
watching you. Pain blunted my instincts.

You would have made such a good father, I thought,
as you ran half-asleep, and mostly naked,
toward the blaze, instinct telling you
someone was dying in there.

Selfie with Wild Mouse Baby

We found a wild mouse baby
just outside the front door.
He was half the size of my thumb.
He was shaking. No mother
mouse and lately the owls
have been caterwauling at dusk.
I named him Garamond
after the delicate font.
He loved milk and lint.
We planned to set him free
the day his eyes opened
but after two nights he died.
He never opened his eyes.
We buried him beside the sunflowers.
Oh Garamond, would a rattlesnake
have done you one better?
Would the snap of an owl
have hurt less
than starving to death
in the cold light
of my fruitless love?

Miss Karen

After the miscarriage I ate pizza
and imagined the tomato sauce as blood
to replace what I had lost.

I went home to Queens to get strong but Karen was
masturbating on the balcony off my old bedroom
and a neighbor came over and said to my mother,

Your son is masturbating on the balcony again.
Then my mother said, Karen is not my son,
and if she were mine, I would call her daughter.

Mom, I'm home because I need something red,
like blood. Karen is in my childhood bed shooting porn.
The balcony off my old bedroom is white wrought iron.

My mother needed another daughter when I moved out,
she was still all red with daughter-love and at night they sit together
at the kitchen table—sucking the iron out of red wine—

my mother and Karen because there are many ways
to love a daughter. They smoke Kent Golden Lights 100s
which are long, long cigarettes and they complain

about the neighbors. When the pizza comes
I remember the miscarriage, what I came to tell my mother,
but why ruin a perfectly good party

when the world is full of people?
I mean, the world is full of pizza.
I mean, the world is full of love.

Thank You Note

Dear Rena, Thank you for your hospitality. I know you're worried about me, but living in my car isn't so bad. I can't invite anyone over, but that means I never have to clean up. LOL. Seriously though, I have the most vivid dreams. My car puts her arms around me and sings me to sleep. She purrs quietly because the parts under the hood are strong. I mean, she has a good heart. When it's freezing out, the car-air tastes like the inside of the refrigerator. I play opera music when I feel afraid. When I need to calm down, it's Verdi. Those oboes in *La Traviata*, they pour liquid gold over me. When I sing along, it's like the car is full of shimmering honey. Have you ever seen the state house in Charleston, West Virginia? That golden dome shines in the sun like you wouldn't believe. It's a magic pill. I want to crush it up and burn it and suck up all the smoke. Living in the car is bad. I could go back to my mother's double-wide, but my brother's back living there with that pill whore. Remember how we used to call you Sputnik, in college, because you were like a little satellite orbiting the Earth? You were always so high. Now you're a professor. You're going to write a whole shelf of books, aren't you? Experimental poetry. Begin at the top. Figure out your coordinates. I am here. Where are you? Prepare for your arrival on Earth: Sputnik, are you ready?

Incarceration

Close like the breath of the truck—
just barely—and
fairness is something
that children imagine,
you become an adult
the day you disavow it.
Sea smoke of disaster
and gravity pulls you
closer to forever.
You're willing to go
but just barely.
When you get
far enough from the Earth
the air becomes something else—
you can still breathe
but just barely.
They built a wall,
put you behind it.
The stars are still here
but you won't be
able to see them
for a number
of your years,
decided by a judge.
You can still breathe
but just barely.

Homeless Ladies Hiding Out at Coastal Coffee Shop During a Rainstorm

I'll call you at the moment day pours into day.
I'll call you when these hands that never heal drag sky.
I'll call before I bait the fish and hide the hook:
Look, there's a place in the keel that collects lightning.
I'll call you when the wind blows all my warmth away.

Fish Disco

Two bullet wounds. Self-inflicted. You left the hospital in a wheelchair. In order to leave, did they make you promise you wouldn't do it again? Next time will someone sell you a gun? How could there be two wounds? Bullet goes in. Bullet goes out. One bang. Two holes. There was a gun in the barn for shooting rats. The rats came when no one tended to the apple trees. All those apples on the ground, it was a party for the rats. It was a feast. So many rats. The apples called the rats. All night the green light that we dropped into the water calls the fish. I call it the fish disco. So many little silver fish move together in waves around the green light. I'm so sorry. The seal came up behind us. We didn't see the seal until the fish were in her mouth. Seals have to eat so many fish every day just to stay fat enough to survive the winter water. Who left the loaded gun in the barn? Are you always going to need that wheelchair? There's something moving in the water behind you, but I can't see what it is.

Freezer Pizza

The apple tree folds over, too many
apples I can't reach and I'm afraid to climb
the ladder if no one will hold the bottom for me.
So the apples will fall, will be food for the bears
and the deer and the family of grey foxes
that walk the ridge at sunset.
They crimp the lacy edge up there,
in the black cut-out that stands in for night
before it is fully dark. I put away the lawnmower.
Another day I didn't mow the lawn. I pull
a pizza out of the freezer. Would the animals
eat this if I left it at the edge of the woods?
Or is it all chemicals? Drugs like the ones I stood for half the day
instead of mowing the lawn or picking the apples
and when I reached the pharmacist,
he gave me a sad look. I'm picking these up
for my husband. I say his name. I say his date of birth.
At sunset the meadow glows golden red
before night covers wildflowers and weeds
with a cold blanket of dark
in order to let the light come from the moon.
In the moonlight I pick at my freezer pizza,
the crimped lacy edge of frozen cheese.
My name. My date of birth. Out the window
the apple tree is exhaling light.

Artifacts

I made this coat from field mice,
I wore it to the city
where a homeless man

yelled in my face, You don't
know what it's like, and
grabbed my fur sleeve.

I pulled a dead mouse
from my pocket and hissed.
I stopped time.

Step into this moment
with me. Here nothing is breathing.
After a mouse gets snapped

the field starts to run again
with small animals, with sap
and stars and coal-black mud.

In the morning the mountain rises,
dances you slow, pulls you over into the green
corner, then locks you out.

In the morning it's just you and the animals
and the mountain. The mist makes it all
just a flat and tall backdrop.

The mist covers from the river
all the ways up the peaks and erases the hills.
For this world they made all the trappings, you know

the museum stuff—the clay figures,
the beads and bowls and bangles and knives.
For this.

Participatory Architecture

What is the name of that shape
when your shelter is just a skeleton—
what's that called? Modern theories

of architecture are called on
to explain families like mine:
I was the flower girl, a minor

part of the participatory architecture
of marriage. It was the happiest
day of my life. We went

from the World's Fair Globe
in Queens to Gottscheer Hall
where the city used to keep us

when we were freshly displaced,
long before I knew the word diaspora.
The World's Fair Globe

stores memories of human behavior:
I was the flower girl in the hoop skirt
at my uncle's wedding. We

gathered at the Globe for pictures.
That Globe is old now, but it came to us
backwards, from the future.

The city is load bearing,
made up of material shapes
and the outlines of absences.

In modern theories of architecture
there is a loss of time. It looks like
circular logic and it goes like this:

We who are used to accepting
the disappearance of family members
find it easier to leave our families.

On Leaving

1

My glamorous grandmother
graduated from beauty school.
Her certificate hangs
on the living room wall
years after she was put in the ground.
They still talk about her, say
she was so smart with that business,
paid under the table where no one can see.

In Gottschee she did farm work,
but not long enough to ruin her
hands. She buried Gottschee
so her memories are mangled:
He picked me to make meat
for the morning, she says.

Grandma and I pick tacky art
in gilded frames to hang over the kitchen table:
a scene of a girl feeding chickens
their morning meat in the woods
beside a thatched hut. That's what
Gottschee was like, she'd tell me.

But she says that about all greeting cards
with rural scenes, and also about the sun setting over
the skyline of Manhattan, and always
when we watch movies about war.

2

Snow comes down loud
off the roof in clumps. Is this how
it sounded in Gottschee, the bombs

I mean, was it like this when the
roof was coming in or was it on fire?
Were the children screaming

and what happened to the chickens?
I've always been told we kept chickens,
but no one seems to know where they went.

3

Tante Sophie was once a little girl
in a refugee camp. There were too many
people in the camp. There was not enough to eat.

Her mother gave her portions to Sophie
and starved to death slowly
while my grandfather walked the map of Europe

to get back to his mother.
When he got there, she was dead.
I have her now inside my body.

She is still starving
no matter how much I feed her.
We eat the map of Europe

to get back the missing pieces.
We swallow countries whole.

4

My grandfather dances back to me in painkiller daydreams
to tell me if I am ever starving, I can
chew the bark off trees, eat the leather off my shoes.

Don't worry, he says. All you need to survive are trees, shoes,
and a slow metabolism. When grandpa's corpse was cold
I touched his face with my chubby little-girl fingers

to make sure he was really dead. Then I went to the bathroom,
whispered tree bark and shoe leather,
took off my white patent leather Mary Janes

and washed them in the sink before putting the more perfect
left shoe into my mouth. My little teeth bit,
but could not rip, could not chew.

Virgin Mary white and blue, what should I do?
Look, she says, all the frightened chickens are surrounded by grace.

5

When my beauty queen
grandmother died,
her body went straight
to the Catholic funeral home
near Gottscheer Hall.
Her head was full of fluids,
swollen to the size of a pumpkin.
They put makeup
on this pumpkin, said it was her,
even as the features of her face collapsed.
In movies, dead
people's faces are
exactly as they are in life,
just perfectly still.
I looked at the cheap flowers, I
smelled the blank crosses of white carnations.
I pressed my face
into my uncle's shoulder
and because of how I shook
everyone thought
I was crying, but no, Grandma's face
made me laugh.
So this is what happens to beauty.

6

Don't concern yourself
with what I eat or where I am.

I know what kind of trap this is.
I am making myself into a ship.

Feel the strength of my hold.
I am packed with provisions

for weeks, months even. I am
turning into the woman in black

at the edge of the woods. There—
you see me and then you blink

and there's nothing to see.

Let Light Come from the Border

Let the borderlight shine you up the mountain
fierce and sweet, rivers and tall trees.
Let the moon stay on the other side of the ice until morning.
Turn down the eyes of the lamp or we will not shine.
Muddy water rounds the curve of the new day.
Let me show you how to stand in the light.

Let the sun suffer a thin green light through the ice.
Let ice chunks stick together to form a large, unstable boat.
Let me show you how to stand in the iceboat without tipping over
as the snow melts down, guided by the moon,
going to the ocean, from where the forest grazes
to where the great white feeds.
Wait for your light.   Wait for your light.

My White Mountains

Up here the wind speeds climb over 200 mph, that's how winter breaks gravity. There's a jewel hidden at the top of the snowy mountain, but the wind blows hikers off the edges before they can see the shine. There's a summer somewhere, maybe that's the shimmering place winter blows hikers into. After they've stopped breathing, winter takes them somewhere warm. Winter cuts down a tree and sets it in my living room. My heart is a model of winter. Winter doesn't last forever for everyone. Winter cracks ice, breaks off at the top, teaches me how to fly, teaches these windy peaks how to play, these snow trap days: search and rescue   melt and rise.

Homeland Security

What if death is the same
as every other border? If you don't know
where you come from, they don't let you cross.

When I left New York City
I was saturated with fear.
Plane crash/ building collapse/

anthrax/ a poison
that shook out of envelopes sometimes.
Remember that? Quietly I sat

on a mountain in the Great North Woods, when the sun
rose and spoke: You will never have a homeland,
she said. I can't give you that.

But I can make your face familiar
so everywhere you go, you will be welcomed home.

Grass, Leaves, Salt, Mud

Each day we are one less day
until the year wins and we begin

like the blackbird with the red arm band
in a high polish of rain,

we miss the night, the nest,
the taproot drinking from the past,

we soar over cows in the mountains
as bears take the pasture

fox for the chickens
all listening to the language of waning light:

happiness the electricity
that keeps us alive in the snow as the stick

of a Hawaiian Punch-flavored lollipop
wilts paper between my teeth, each night

we take double electricity,
until the moon wins, seasons the prize,

each with a distinct stain: grass,
leaves, salt, mud.

First the Fan

First the fan of baseball fields, then the blotchy geometries of farms
in winter,
then the clouds, the clouds and only the clouds, this one so thick
it's all there is to see/ the clouds and the wing
with its blue triangle fin spearing out at the sky/ bearing us
somehow home
to the urban mists of New York in winter.
You will go on to Maine and I will wake Christmas morning
alone/ until
we meet halfway/ in the in-between
where the Connecticut River splits Vermont from New Hampshire.
I can't tell if we're still over Indiana or maybe that's Cleveland/
the captain
makes an announcement and we squint
as though we could squint the clouds clear/ we pretend to make out
what's down there.

Buffalo, the captain says, Buffalo
and thirty-five to forty minutes from JFK, we found a bit of
smooth air.
It may get rough later, he says. Earlier he used the phrase "bumpy
air"/ I like his words.
You point me to a footnote in your book; representation is a
good word
you say, we are too close to each other to write poetry and
read theory:
sprung, the footnote says, means uprising, in German,
and we are rising up/ through the clouds/ I point down at Buffalo
and it looks like the snow is shimmering up through the air with
hallucinatory grace.

Snow uprising./ Snow sprung./ Sprung snow.
I'm dreaming of a White Christmas/ I'm glad we're not going
to Buffalo
a city we've been through, but it never stopped us, never made us
shiver with awe.

I think the stewardess is too old for this job. I want to hold her in
my arms,
make her young again. Someone's kid
screams. Someone always brings a kid that screams, to remind you
that youth is pain.

Down there it's no longer Buffalo, now it's mountains
and white lines where trees were eliminated
so skiers can cut their own rows.
Mountain ridges like curvy ladies
laying down beside each other, singing:
lay-lady-lay, like Bob Dylan
as they sigh and roll over and rearrange themselves when no one
is looking.
The wing is glinting sun like the arms of a ringmaster covered
in rhinestones:
Behold! This land is your land/ layers of imperfect rivers and roads
and farms in fans.
When I was a child I believed these outlines were the outlines
of states,
and all the divisions were finally revealing themselves,
and there was no such thing as representation.

I can see it now: that frozen lake is Arkansas
and there/ that must be Nebraska/ I'd know that boxy blue
wasteland anywhere.
Then America dissolves into rows of roofs and swimming pools.

There's the Connecticut River like a snake/ so long it goes to the
horizon rainbow
and all the way to Long Island herself, a careful fish
with the city in her eye/ looking at the snake river
that wants to bite her head off
but can't seem to fit that snake mouth
around all those tall buildings and so many train lines:
impossible iron spaghetti strands
that can't be cut and are too numerous to count.

Wake up! The city is spellbound
I tell you, Look! Look at the pollution, like some sort of brown prayer
the city collects around herself. Wake up! We're here.
Circling water so low the birds
chatter at us/ they watch and fly
as we swirl and we touch down.

Ridgewood

wanted to give you something
that you could use forever
long after you left
and built a replica of the city in a shoebox.

In Queens your mother
makes goulash that stains
the staircase hallway
with a permanent brown smell.

In her shoebox apartment
everything is made from
something else being turned inside out
and it all lasts forever.

At the table you learned
to read off the back of a milk carton.
Missing children peered out at you.
The word "missing" didn't make sense

in your context so you changed its meaning
to something more like used,
used up, used again, born again, begin again.
In Queens the refugees begin again.

Firebreak

One summer's night
listening in French
we watched fireworks
from a castle's old
stone bench. Once
you were a boy on
a pony in a childhood
gritty with stars. I used to
email sonnets to myself,
blind herds of symbols
and sheep. In the spring
bears dance down my
dreams. In the glitter
of winter, salt calls
the moose to the roads.
In the dangerous heart
of New Hampshire
black-iced birches bow
to admire the slick highway.
You smelled happiness
last night in the woodsmoke
that got stuck in your hair.
This morning the coffee
smells like burning, but darker.
The aurora borealis
danced over
the party last night.
At the fire station,
the birds assembled
and sang. Birds are important.
You find them in every
definition of freedom.
Last night was like
New England but brighter.
The fire broke

on a young gleam.
The fire always breaks
with a little glitter.
You held up your phone
and that's when you saw it:
a purple light in the sky,
edged with green.
Tonight the sunset
will just be a glowing shape
in the rear-view mirror.
Who are you to be desperate?
The rock in your heart
is just a shape. When
you break you do not glow.
That's what a firebreak
is for: you stop the fire.
Tell me you understand me.
You do not let the fire
near the house.

Logical Legacies

If everything melts
then the houses resume
the truth of their shapes.
If porticos and transom windows,
then French doors and bird baths.
If rectangles in the ice, then triangles in the sky.
Geometries strictly surface, I've got
feedback loops, I've got inheritance anxiety,
I've got beer, wine and the harder stuff.
I've got infinite external hardware
melting in escrow, too real
real estate and property taxes
peel to taste and pepper the soup.
If the trees start to bug again
in the cold washes of Maine
and in the clean green wastes
of New Hampshire, and if everything melts,
then the houses can resume
their strict surface geometries
and their inherited feedback
loops, called legacies.
If everything blooms
then the house may collapse,
then make an inventory
of land, property, legacy,
and oh, by the way, how much cash
is stashed in this apartment?
If there's cash in the utensils
drawer (it won't close) and if there's cash
curled up in the coffee mugs,
then there's cash hidden in the walls.
Help me find it.

No One On This Road But Us and the Night

1

There's no one on this road but us and the night, you say.
The bugs are invisible and everywhere: summer.
Winter will naturally debug the kitchen,
but tonight I need a drive.

You said your father would drive you around when you were sleepless,
together you'd cruise the night roads of Maine. I imagine
if you were sleeping when you got home, he carried you in,
closed the door with his foot. I imagine the weight of your boy body

held. I believe an idea can have weight before words:
I was with you there, though I wasn't a body, but a math.
Black and white headshots of old movie stars
somehow always look familiar. It must be an algorithm.

2

It's the clothing my soul wears, I say, picking at my skin.
On television they are running races.
The code you are looking at is not the code that is running.
On television Gidget is surfing.

Change the station: an anesthetized alligator
goes into the bag like a body bag.
The options are: copy/distribute/modify:
or take me home/ in kind.

3

In our strange extinction history/ we are on the chapter of death:
in a rainforest there's only that one pretty math

and it goes into the bag like a body bag.
On television the refugees are drowning.

The code you are looking at
is not the code that is running.

I can see you sometimes as a little boy, there are ways you turn,
and your boy-self flickers on. Hit save.

Boathouse

I carved my name into the boathouse
in the morning, right here,
the first spot the sun touches.
Every boathouse has a secret

to keep in the morning, written first
in the language of early light.
Meet me here at the boathouse
at dawn and I will show you how
to build a boat: how to shape the hull like shoulders,
how to sing the paintbrush over the heart of the prow.

Here, I was here, my name remains here, pressed down
into this old wood. Show me where your name is.
You picked the spot where the wood siding touches the soil.
You picked the place where the darkness falls first.

Spring Shanty

Pull magnolia leaves from the scuppers,
drain the water from the cockpit,

grab the spare orange life preserver,
take the tiller and put in the cotter pins.

Go through the chain plates,
check the mast, the standing rigging,

lower the upper shrouds. Make certain
of the forestay, the backstay and the husband

as he leans our aluminum ladder up
against the side of the sailboat. Unzip

the door in the protective plastic.
Climb in. Boats dream of the smack

and tang of salt, the force of the rudder
against the waves. Inside the winter plastic

the air smells of sun-warm tarpaulin
and the faint low note of epoxy. The boat

knows my husband by his hands, as
they are part of the early spring melt,

the rise and the swim, when the sun birds
fly home and the fish school back to us.

Pearls

Now we are back at the house on Brackett Street/ and I have all our
shells and seaglass
and driftwood/ spread out on the back porch table/ and one big jar/
and the love of my life
is in the kitchen/ scraping barnacles off muscles with a butter knife.

This jar will keep the sea with us. On the table is the camera
with its one twist-closed eye/ pointed straight up/ hawk-watching.

The cork from last night's bottle/ 24 pieces of beach glass
a foot of clean, blonde driftwood/ 11 shells
3 rocks and a bag of sand/ the smell

of mussels in garlic comes steaming out of the kitchen.
You come/ pick up the best one/ you say, this is the most beautiful
rock I have ever seen.
Children ride by/ ringing the bells on their bicycles.

I suck the barnacle cuts on your fingers/ the trees in the backyard
clap their millions
of leaves/ you put on a record/ the white album/ and sand sails off
the porch
onto the green lawn, kept summer-people perfect/ Only one refused
to open!

You yell./ Wonderful./ These old barnacled-up mussels still have
something in them:
the ocean music/ what it refuses
and the tree music of oxygen making.

The mussels are full of pearls.
I swallow them/ thinking they are rocks.
I am too in love with you to care.

Part Three: The Encrypted Latina

Over Jackson Heights

The sun rose white
while the subway counted out
blue rosary beads.

A Story About Birds

Tell me a story about birds, Abuela,
to make sense of the ghosts that heal us

with song. Extinct birds can't ever come home
but their ghosts will sing like Abuela did:

come-home songs for places that no longer exist.
Out on the open ocean, birds land on our boat, worn-out

with the unspeakable exhaustion of migration.
Their eggs are full of poison, that means

the new birds are sicker than the old birds.
Abuela's ghost teaches me come-home songs.

I sing, but no animal responds. No warbler, sparrow,
not even the whales, those famous singers. In dreams

silence hides inside the birds. Ghosts slip
across the border. I sing the come-home song

and nothing comes. I dream the American dream:
each night armed men break into my house,

they barge up the stairs, arrest me, put me in
a cage. This has to do with my country, with my home,

with the unspeakable exhaustion of migration.
Abuela, tell me a story about birds.

Chango

All the girls in my paintings wear gas masks
and pretend they are not afraid. I make voodoo
dolls to bring the wrath of Chango on the girls
in gym class who hurt me. How discreetly
I steal strands of their hair, how studiously
I invent incantations. My mother doesn't understand
when she finds the careful dolls, even when I tell her
what they say about our family: Send them all back.
They call us criminals. One girl gets a pin in each eye,
and the second gets a paperclip tight
around her neck. But first I paint the toenails,
the nipples, the anus—all with the same candy pink
nail polish. Then I take a black marker
and draw a six-foot man on the shell pink
wall of my bedroom. He is just an outline,
but he's got a semi-automatic weapon.
It's not that he's bad. He's just had enough. Don't you understand?

The Encrypted Latina

1: Syllogism

This is how I use logic
to justify when Abuela calls
all blonde American actors

Leonardo DiCaprio:
If we take x to mean actor
and actor to mean Leonardo DiCaprio;

then x equals Leonardo DiCaprio.
That's a syllogism. Now
if we take Jude Law to mean actor

and actor to mean Leonardo DiCaprio
then Jude Law equals Leonardo DiCaprio
and Abuela is not wrong

when she tells me not to waste my time
dreaming about blonde American actors.

2: Recursion

Two mirrors facing each other
in a beauty parlor
that is also a kitchen

in a life paid for
one manicure at a time
exfoliating the faces

of the newest New Yorkers
pressing hair into curlers
or permanents or

removing hair
that gets an old woman
mistaken for an old man.

One mirror faces the other: a box of
infinity in our little corner of Queens.

3: Feedback Loop

The robin puffs up at the sight of his own reflection puffing up.
Then he goes for it, chest-first hitting the glass
at 5AM again and again. I wake, then go outside,

to save him. To wave him away with a broom.
He's afraid of me but keeps coming for himself. The sun rises
and there I am, in my robe at 5AM, thinking about how

skinny people make me feel fat, but when I'm saving the robin
I'm a different person. The hero of my own story.
Strong and stubborn I am just like him:

a modern puffed-up protagonist, I keep coming at my own
reflection. Chest-first I swing the broom—
the sound is the worst part, the whoosh of air cutting the sunrise.

I don't want the robin to die looking at himself, thinking *enemy*.
I drop the broom. I sing the world's saddest song.

You Will Know Us by Our Song

Celia Cruz sang *Guantanamera*
like Abuela used to, before that tube
went down her throat, before the hanging
bags of medicine—fruit from the metal tree—
ripened and fed her. I see you, metal tree.
What hurts is the lack of roots. Refugees
are trees that live on air, root to music,
prayer, family, food, and all together
it becomes a sort of feedback loop: Celia

Cruz sang *Guantanamera* and I sang
along, loud—I was wearing a mask, but I
wanted Abuela to hear me. My lips
close to her ear. I sang loud, bent over
the plastic walls of the hospital bed.
My hips did a small dance. My feet pranced.
Were her feet moving? Was she in the past, dancing?
Abuela, can you hear me?

Oye Como Va came on, the doctor
came in and I did not see him and I
love that song, so I sang loud as I could.
When the doctor walked in he saw me:
a thirty-five-year-old woman dressed for
a party singing *Oye Como Va*
to her Abuela in the middle of the night.

Once, when I taught yoga, I played Chinese flute
music for my class. There was a bird just
outside the window, the bird recognized
something in the music and sang along.

That night, the doctor who came into the room
with me and Abuela, he recognized
the song, and in beautiful Spanish, he began to sing.

Do Not Be Afraid

Two little girls, braided and brown,
sat beside me hugging their grandfather
next to my husband as the boat pushed
through the froth toward the swells
that might be whales, but weren't, not yet.
Their grandfather wore a thick sweater
like my husband did that day and they
nodded at each other as if to acknowledge
that out of all the things in this great world
to wake up early for, whale watching
wasn't even in the top ten. Then the whales
started leaping two by two, beside the boat,
under the double rainbow, the grandfather
started hollering and pointing—suddenly the whales
were all around us—the little girls shrieked,
and I began to cry, I didn't know it until
I turned my face to my husband's chest
and I was wiping good wet tears
and salt on his sweater. Then I pulled away—
more whales had arrived and in their spray
was my dead grandmother, yes, I saw her—young!
Using the breath whales shoot above the surface,
she said, Do not be afraid. She said,
You have been grieving long enough.

Alternate Ending: The Old Man and the Sea

The Virgen de la Caridad del Cobre shows up,
inhales the pain off the fisherman's hands,
exhales an angel to kiss his mouth.

The ocean around Cuba
is teeming with angels.
They clot the air.

Hemingway only saw sharks,
knew Jesus as splinters, he called it luck
when the angels held

his boat against the waves. Called it sun,
when the warm rays sent by the Virgen
de la Caridad del Cobre browned his face.

Maybe only Cubans can see her,
no matter where we are in the world.

Sweet Sixteen

All the cheerleaders gathered at the Knights of Columbus Hall on Long Island, but first we dressed each other, hair-sprayed and lip-sticked, we drank and smoked. Then it was time. Caribbean food gingered and glistened in aluminum trays, there was a DJ and the girls wore tight dresses to the boys in baggy pants.

A teenage boy mouthed to another teenage boy who pulled a gun to his gun and they stood while everyone else got quiet and another cheerleader pulled me under the table and I wasn't worried about getting shot—the boys only had eyes for each other—no, it was the catered food I worried about, the costs: the rented hall, the DJ, the new dresses. All spoiled. Then the matriarch got up on a chair and said: *if you got beef, take it outside.*

But what about all the real beef in the trays?

They went outside, the boys. Then the police came and we all left. What happened to the food? The hall, the DJ, the dresses, they couldn't afford it, but—

What happens to a girl in the ruins of her rites of passage?
Children of refugees, like me
and her, and half the cheerleaders—

waiting for the shot—
after sixteen years of what *we can't afford,*
it's all there now, to spoil and to rot.

Orozco and the Disco Queen

In the basement of the big library next door/ the Orozco murals come alive/ and talk to the ghosts of Wheelocks and Websters past. They peer in the windows of your dreary kitchen and tell you not to waste your time dedicating all your damn poems. The dead don't care/ the living don't notice.

Your kitchen poems always burn anyway/ the smell gets caught in your hair. Tonight each word gets a quick microwave minute. You are addicted to the cheap cook of the microwave. Once you thought you could kill yourself by holding your breath. You woke up in a hospital in Trinidad with big dark ants crawling up the walls/ argued your way out and flew back to the United States the next morning. You went straight from the airport to fill up a shopping cart in the harsh rectangle bright yellow cat-eye supermarket/ you inhaled so sharply the label flew off the can you were holding

right into your mouth. It tasted like wood and like melting. You can have anything you want/ the ghosts said, so you danced all night at the disco party and then took a beautiful stranger back to your basement room. Of course, the Wheelock and Webster ghosts looked away politely, but Orozco's ghosts danced right through you.

How Abuelo Died

A nanoparticle of gold/ in solution/ looks red
because of plasma. Let's call that plasmonic red.
The multinanoscalpel causes budding, causes springtime.
Surgery on a cell that is still living? *Stand by me.*

It's important not to kill the cell. Nanoparticles
do not break. The cells are growing orange.
The water is heating by lattice heat transfer.
Raquel Welch is in a yellow submarine
in your brain/ blasting tumors/ with lasers.
Stand by me.

Are these particles toxic?
Why are they greenish like gaslight?
Raquel Welch uses that laser very well.
What can we do with this model?

We can turn the plasma on/ we can turn the plasma off.
The purple phenomenon/ of a plasmonic structure,
you must use Maxwell's equation to see it:

many scientific careers were made trying to impress Raquel Welch.
Life is just a dream. The dislocation is decided.

Consider the transfection of cells in gene therapy:
put the gene you want to transfect into the
virus and the virus
does the job. HIV with excluded DNA
would be perfect, but the FDA
won't let us try on the human body. So we have movies.

When a sex symbol smiles on us
small scientists will dream cellular subjectivity
and someday, they
will transfect the shit out of it.

When the night has come, when the night has come,
and the cells are still living, even at a 65% perforation rate.
No I won't be afraid.

I See You, Gilet Jaunes

The hospital lobby
is the best part.
Leather couches,
glass rotating doors,
big-screen TVs
all soberly turned
to the news—like it matters
what is happening
outside this hospital.
The Gilet Jaunes
in France are
vandalizing their own
cities. I love their
poetic graffiti:
Nous sommes rien
(We are nothing)
Nous voulons tout
(We want everything)

Isn't that how we all feel?
Especially in this hospital
in Queens, New York,
where the heat goes out at night
in the middle of the winter.
My ninety-four-year-old abuela
yells, *Frio! Frio!*
That means cold.
Too cold for a dying
Cuban refugee. I grab
the last extra blanket
from the nurses.
The next woman
who asks for a blanket
is told there are no more.

We are nothing.
We want everything.

Kindle No Fires

1: Rena's Name

Rena lives with ghosts, like all children of refugees. The wind says boo, then clicks at the window until she gets up and slams it closed—fuck you.

Rena writes a note to be read in the event of her death: *Turn me into ashes when I die. Don't dare bury me alive, or I will come back and ruin your happiness. My ghost will be silent and brutal because my name was dreamed up in a jail cell.*

2: Esperanza's Name

If Esperanza can say her name out loud before the ghosts get to her, if she can remember the lilt of lullabies, if she can bite the hand at her throat, if the hand will ooze real blood, then this incarceration is not a dream. Wake up; this is a prison.

It's the guards who come for her name. This can't be Cuba, she tells herself, she must call it something else. This can't be my life, she says. She is living someone else's hell. Nights she makes lists of names that could belong to the woman whose life this is, she tries to name the woman this is really happening to, while men pry the gold from her teeth.

I'm not dead yet, she protests. They ask for names and she says every first name she can think of, until she knows the shape of every possible name—they all fit in her toothless mouth—but which one is hers?

3: Joan

Become Joan of Arc
incline toward the sharp sun,
heed the seashore's one sign:

Kindle no fires.
That means keep your clothes on.
No licking salt from skin.

Whetstones keep
my heart sharp at the edges
and Joan's skin still burns.

4: Chiquita Banana

Abuela dances with Abuelo on the beach every night in her dreams, doesn't matter that he's dead. Jesus wraps them in his arms of light and all the angels are there, dancing. They've invited me to dance with them, calling me up: Rena, you gotta get down here, the beach is radiant with your displaced dead.

When I arrive, they are all so happy to see me. We cha-cha-cha close to the foam lace the ocean makes when she licks the sand with her wet burning salt tongue.

I have all of Esperanza's teeth in my mouth. She tells me to keep them—she doesn't need teeth. She slobbers on a cigar stuck between her gums and she wears a fruit hat like Chiquita Banana.

The music we dance to in this dream comes from her tape player. These days she's an angel over the church parades, whispering questions into the ears of dressed-up little girls, still looking for her name.

El Esqueleto Humano

The tree shape inside the body that disappears when we sleep, the
bone-trap rippling out
over the dark surface like a keening wolf:

squirrel trap, rat trap, snap-trap, rope-trap, hole-in-the-ground then
building the fire
crunch of bone in teeth, means pulling gristle apart, means
scavengers who make nests out of bones
and feathers or a husband striking the back of a truck,
shadowboxing a silent boneless hulk

means architecture until it breaks, a shot deer hung on a hook,
bleeding from the neck then field dressing,
cotton and suede, shirtless superhero of Idaho, the first rule of
Adam and Eve, one woman and one man,
and everybody else is somewhere in-between, means she
bleeds rainbows

means doctoring the chicken long enough and then deciding one
day to have it for lunch,
means cling peaches that make us think of how muscles cling to
bone until the day they don't,
when the bones turn to swords inside the body

means beatings that pull us out of our dreams
and I hope he clips her wings, the other-side neighbor says

means making a skeleton from cigarettes
means rinsing hands with pink foam soap and blood disappearing
down the drain,
means a crown of chicken bones and feathers woven together into a
bird bone basket,
means building the fire, then burning her dresses
which the neighbors will see as a vast light

Last Night in Jackson Heights

Last night in Jackson Heights, Ecuador was in season and I sat on the balcony and let the wind blow Spanish at me while I read poems in German and I felt like Rilke was touching my hair and I imagined an ecstatic Ecuadorian Jesus winning the World Cup.

This morning on Park Avenue, I have the Santa Barbara feeling.

He had a stigma on his face, says the man at the table next to mine. I have been that man. I mean, I am hungry for stigma and soccer and no matter who wins tonight, Queens will light up and I'll stand on the balcony and cheer and then the loudest car will pull up below and scream for me to flip up my shirt and show my breasts to the kings of the country of soccer.

How would Rilke answer them? Rilke would think they were angels. Dumb shit.

What am I saying? I love Rilke.

See how the dead are clumped here but just past the far fence they are laid out in rows? None of these accommodations are spacious but they keep the dead still. In Queens my people live among graveyards. Hold your breath while we pass. Some of these still have lanes for hearses to drive through, and some have covered over the lanes with additional graves.

You can't tell a swim from a suicide jump just by looking at the bridge. It has to do with surfacing, with whether or not you are holding your breath.

You tell a different story when you are not sitting at the bar. You know by the way he looks at you. The police walk by checking their guns. I am looking at their bodies. The waitress forgot my order. Someone walks by who looks like my first best friend. Sometimes the people who pass stare back but they don't see me. They see my mother or my credit card number or their first best friend. When I perform, people come just to stare into my eyes.

I would never Google you, my mother says.

I would never do such a thing, says my credit card.

Bears Protect the Town

When my sister was arrested, I was on a small plane
to Miami, ears stuck with pearls/ given to me the day

of silk and white lace/ the moment I said, I do.
Like a disheveled debutante on a jet, let's go:

bride-like nervousness when my documents were torn
photographs taken (away) today it is legal to leave,

tomorrow it will not be. Tomorrow brought news of her arrest
and began eighteen years of not knowing—is my sister dead?

Yesterday I was sure she was dead, but today
she's alive again. I encrypted my talk, blacked out

parts of letters that mention her name,
blotted her out of my thoughts for the sake

of my ordinary soul. This summer there are so many foxes,
my granddaughter says. And this is code too.

The bears protect the town, she continues, eyes wide.
Not code. A mistake/ she speaks Spanish poorly.

Her town in New Hampshire hosts a bear sanctuary.
If only Cuba had bears in the mountains instead of men

who turned against God. I tell my granddaughter:
they went up talking about Jesus

but when they came down, Castro was the new king.
No Christmas. If only we had bears for protection then!

On my 90th birthday my sister comes from Miami.
Alive. She made it to Florida. I never asked how.

In Miami my sister makes tapes
of church music from street parades. She got on a plane by herself

because Jesus told her she must. When my sister shook her shoulders
in those shirts, she was music. Doesn't know how to work

the sewing machine, telephone, typewriter, computer.
Only a tape deck. I remember her in tailored dresses.
Spangled shirts in pink and baby blue.
I want to give my granddaughter

the old life/ but all she wants to talk is bears.
She's never had a sister/ mambo back from the dead.

My mirrors face each other/ \showing infinity/ \Jesus is everywhere:
the silk flowers and the ceiling cracks/ the pigeons shitting on the sill.

I used to get up to chase them away, until arthritis crippled my hands
made me see the pigeons are Jesus keeping company with me.

The only thing I can clearly remember from my own incarceration
in the psych ward at Payne Whitney Manhattan

was watching the sun go down/ over twenty lanes of traffic.
I drove all the cars. The rush of thousands of gas pedals pressed,

made me strong enough to swim to Cuba/ Break back in
to the old world. Parade music wafts up from the past.

I've never driven a car or held a weapon
so I may need to rely on the kindness of bears.

Girl from Guantánamo

American abuses ruined the name/ of the most Cuban song you know.
You love it anyway. You played it at the wedding
for Abuela. You want to learn to play the cello.
At the wedding there was a cellist/ and dancing. You can't afford a cello

so you painted one/ life-sized on canvas/ this will keep you
faithful to the idea of getting a real cello/ faithful to the music
    of marriage:
new instruments making old sounds.
Right now it is enough/ to look at the cello painting/ and listen to
    Yo-Yo Ma,

it is enough/ to listen to Celia Cruz/ and smile Abuela's smile.
It is like having a cello.
It is like having a Cuba.
You see someone with the same face as your dead lover

walking the street on a Cuban afternoon—it's just someone who
    looks like him,
but your eyes turn into hungry mouths—and you look and look,
you feel prickly-alive for the first time in all the grieving years/ just
    look, look,
pretend you can undo death/ like putting on a record in reverse

making the world spin the wrong way
so he could dance backwards into your arms/ whispering *mi vida,*
    mi vida…

Speeding Down the Long Island Expressway

Cigarette butts crushed on the narrow edges
of sidewalks beset with dirty island roses.
Anxiety. Candy. Cigarettes. Yes, please.

Rain came suddenly, race-you-to-the-car
on the way home from the beach, we'd smoke
and drink iced coffees. My polished toes on the dashboard,

my mother cranked the radio—that song—
gave my smooth shins goosebumps
and I made fun of her for not knowing the words.

Sand lodged in the cracks of the scratchy leather seats.
You have to learn the words, I insisted, and sang too loud,
speeding until we got pulled over—I'll need to see your license

and registration. I was a blue flower. Do you know why
I pulled you over today? My mother was a flame.

I Love Windows

His relatives are shocked
by my smile. Nice to meet you, I say.
It hasn't hit her yet,

they murmur. She's in shock, they say.
Mike had told me years of family secrets
and now they're all here, dressed in black.

Before he killed himself, Mike washed and folded his clothes.
He cleaned his room. He baked his mother a pie.
It will be ok, Mike's grandmother gently

tells me. Then she hands me a cookie
big with chocolate chips, from a bright blue and white
French porcelain plate. Today the police are gone,

replaced by family. There is something
wrong with this cookie. It's like a prop.
It's not real. It doesn't have a taste or smell.

It's crying outside, the wet trees shake
with tears, blow and break, but I am inside, sitting still,
eating a beige cookie on a chocolate-chip sofa. I wonder,

have I ever really loved anyone?
I know I love cookies, for their sugar. I love windows,
for their suggestion of escape.

The Spider Called Maman

after Louise Bourgeois

She grew so large I could see her egg sac
even in the brick and iron portico where Mike told me
life without my love wouldn't be worth the pain.

We left pale white filaments behind us
but they became strong invisible webs and the rope for his neck
while I worried about bright tangibles: my scholarship, my hair.

If I didn't go to class, the giant
spider would find me. But Mike stopped going to class
and then he moved into the egg sac. Then

I broke up with him.   Then he was dead.
I won't say how he did it. Won't paint
a suicide, but after Mike took his last breath,

the spider got up and walked. The campus
was marked with her tracks those first nights of fragrant spring rain.
Don't look at the spider now; she's standing still.

She's pretending it never happened.
Let's remember Mike like this:
It's twilight in that cold romantic portico

and the ground is wet with springtime and smudged cigarettes.
We are smoking marijuana when he looks up at the spider and says,
I get it, but why do we have to call her Mother?

I respond with: What makes art
worth what it's worth? It doesn't matter
what you call her, I said, it's written

in the imprint of her footsteps
it's there in the tone of her voice
when she says   Love costs too much.

Seeing Each Other

The TV was too loud when you stopped breathing.
Your little sister couldn't sleep. Your mother broke down
the door in the morning, two years ago. Your mother found you.

My stubborn love
makes a new sense for you,
like eyesight I know
you've been watching me swim summers
down the river, under the bridge, and older
than you ever were.

You saw the little black dress
I described when they asked the inevitable:
What were you wearing?
I hadn't slept with anyone
since you. I kept my vigil.

That night, almost exactly two years after your death, you watched.
That's the problem with heaven. You were the only witness
when I was on my back and begging him to stop.
I know you saw because I saw you die again.

Hungerstrike

1

We can look at pictures of your brain
together, you said,

but I got a strong drink
instead of keeping my MRI appointment.

Mike's death was made of glass
I can see clear through it

to the silent middle nightmareplace
in the middle of the night.

Girls are bad at math, except lesbians.
Being bad at math costs too much.

Being a woman costs too much,
I'm not going to buy any of it anymore.

We're all on payroll, but you darling have everything
white-man-worth and young and you.

I am worth less—a woman of
mixed blood: half-Cuban/half-crazy.

Today you went to see
about your car—the one you can't afford anymore.

I don't care what it looks like, I tell you.
But some nights you watch me change my clothes five times;

This looks stupid…This looks stupid…
Does this make me look fat?

(No darling, I say, no one is allowed in for a look at my brain.
Let's live heavy and uncertain.)

I don't want to know what's wrong,
please don't let that mean we will always be afraid.

When my favorite homeless man, who goes by Waterhead,
stopped me on 14th Street and 3rd Avenue and asked

why I was crying
I just kept walking.

When Mike died in the middle of the night, I was 19.
I can learn how to live on the other side watching, but why?

Later on that afternoon I felt bad for ignoring Waterhead
and I sat beside him on the warm subway grate

that lifts his meaty and old stale marijuana smoke smell
above the cold sidewalk. He asked me if I wanted to get high

and I said, No, and then I said Waterhead, what do you want?
What do you really want, more than anything?

He puffed a little on his joint to get it started,
and smiled and said strawberrymilk,

and we sat there in the pink glow of the word.

2

When I got home to you, darling, we climbed
up the ladder to the roof and I thought (like I always do) about jumping

(it has to look like an accident or else
everyone will blame themselves)

as you smoked a joint beside me and asked where
I wanted to go to dinner.

How about a hungerstrike?
How can we eat, darling?

Tell me how to taste the bread
baked in the ovens this war keeps hot

and wouldn't you like
me better if I stopped eating?

But Sally my psychiatrist says,
Rena, you must let yourself

have this relationship,
so instead I say,

Baby, what do you want?
What do you really want, more than anything?

And you smoked that joint hard, frowning
into your exhales, and then you answered;

I want to be there for you in the middle
of the night. And if I can't be, I want

you to not feel so much sadness and loss.
The sun was going down

and we sat there in the pink glow of the world.

The Planting Fields

On the Gatsby Coast there's an outdoor dollhouse sized to fit the grief of a child. There is a mansion too, but it is unimportant. The North Shore of Long Island is lined with gold. The homeless man said: I specialize in problem recognition. I use previously-solved problems and apply a previously-developed solution. No. That's not what the homeless man said. I said no, I will not marry you. A string is a sequence, strings are immutable; lists are mutable, why didn't we use a list?

He criticized my syntax, my methods, my invocations. The Gold Coast is littered with old mansions no one lives in. Mike didn't want to take the tour. He never intended to get old. He tried to convince me not to go back (take love as a parameter) to college. He took me to the Planting Fields to ask me to marry him; he proposed just outside of the dollhouse (take a knee) not the mansion, and it was clear: that we were the dolls, I mean, we were kids, playing. That's why I said no.

Two nights before Mike died we went to the beach. We ate sushi that night, and we lived on Long Island. I called his phone on the dead morning because there was a sink dripping my heart and I couldn't turn it off. When a stranger picked up his phone and I said my own name I knew. His sister called me back. I knew nothing

(take suicide as a parameter)

she said words. Nothing. I said words/ I said nothing. Maybe I said: The North Shore of Long Island is old gold for the asking. Or she said: How close is close enough?

Today it's ten years later. Today there's a homeless man in the town by the sea where my husband and I have found a café to do Sunday things. The homeless man is attracted to my husband and he says: Be humble and be kind. She will worship you for the rest of your life. The homeless man wears a wool hat even though it's August. He calls a cab and when it comes, he tells the driver he's got nowhere to go. He gets a cup of coffee for free and it's basically a miracle: fishes and loaves from his fingertips. On the way out of the café he stops at our table again, to sniff and spread his wings like a seagull, and he says: We're all going to heaven, so don't worry about that.

We're all going to heaven. I agree, but not because we are good. It's because we are stuck in a loop in which the terminating condition is never satisfied.

Various Roosters

1: The Shot

The shot is close and loud.
It sounds like he fired
inside in that cavernous old barn.

We never heard a gunshot
coming from the neighbor's side
of the street before.

It was surprising to think
he owned a gun, his land
was posted: NO HUNTING.

We had never spoken to him
and neither of us wanted to go over
so we didn't. No excuses

needed to be invented.
We simply pretended
it did not happen. And maybe

nothing did happen. What if
it was a car backfiring
or someone hunting illegally?

Going over to the other
side of the road
is unthinkable. Even if he's dead,

the rules seem clear:
if he didn't invite us
over when he was alive

he would not want us
poking around now.
And of course he's still alive, right?

But how would we know if he wasn't?
Would hawks circle the house?
Would the coy dogs set up and howl all night?

2: Credible Threats

Now Roger Federer is speaking
and I'm sitting in the highest faculty row
on the stage. My bags are packed,

in the car. In my mind
I'm already in Stockholm,
sipping coffee on a dock.

Now I get a whiff of mothballs.
These robes and regalia
are packed away every other day of the year.

It's not like we can wear them to a party.
There are thousands of people
in folding chairs sitting on the green.

The people in the chairs and the people
on the stage are boxed in by police officers.
Some are wearing riot gear. And then

there are the police that we can't see.
Have there been credible threats today?
How many? Typically the stage isn't boxed in

on the sides with metal fencing.
I know it's meant to keep us safe
to keep out those who would hurt us,

but it also keeps us penned in, doesn't it?
That's the way safety works. You have to
trade away some of your freedoms.

We watch and wonder who might be hiding a gun.
Am I the only one whose hands
start to tremble when a cop gets too close?

3: Various Roosters

If someone came to this event intending to kill people,
would they point the gun at the stage or at the crowd?
More people are on the lawn, but all the roosters are up here,

clad in robes with fanciful sleeve accents denoting their status,
and puffy hats. I would say being up here today is pretty risky.
Wish I'd thought about it before. Instead I was putting snacks

in the sleeves of my gown. I put almonds and apples
and a bottle of water in there. It's a long ceremony.
Knowing I have snacks gives me comfort, but now I try to configure

my face so that if someone were shooting, they wouldn't want to
shoot me. Does it help that I'm a woman? Does it help
that I'm Latina? The world is full of Latinas but in the faculty section

of the graduation stage at Dartmouth College,
it seems Latinas are in short supply.
I mean, it's me and one other lady. That's it.

Does this mean I am more visible and therefore more likely to get shot?
I rub off my red lipstick with the back of my hand.
I'm ready to leave this country.

4: Protocol

Roger Federer
is talking about tennis.
I am two years younger
than him. It feels
like we are in a play.
He is the star
and I am a part
of the scenery,
a silent tree
or a velvet curtain.
Is my neighbor dead?

In the front row
of the student section
there are four empty seats
that hold tasteful arrangements
of white flowers in glass vases.
They sit there in memory
of four students
who died
during their time
as undergraduates.
Most were suicides.
Is my neighbor dead?

And what exactly
is the protocol
if someone shoots at us?

What if someone
shoots at the stage
and I don't get hit?

Would it be ok
to go to the airport,
and fly to Stockholm?

5: Snacks

I'm sitting up on the stage
with the television star
and the tennis pro
and the college president
who says that the students
who came to talk with her
about the protests and the arrests
brought food to the meeting,
because they wanted her
to feel nourished. This
reminds me that my sleeves
are full of snacks. I pull out
the bag of almonds and rip it open.
This is a mistake. Almonds
fly everywhere. The faculty
sitting around me stiffen
and scowl. Not my husband.
He cheerfully grabs an almond
off the hat of the man sitting
in front of him and pops it
in his mouth with a wink.
I text him: Is our neighbor dead?
He responds: Of course not.

6: Various Roosters

I have seen roosters
barking at dogs in the morning. Are
they trained to attack
or do they just wake up
angry? I have seen roosters
work the earth with their claws.
I have seen roosters
primping their feathers.

Are there roosters who ignore
the dawn? Are there roosters who
prefer to celebrate midnight?

They say the rooster knows
when it is going to rain.
Rooster, you have no obligation to tell me anything,
but if you wanted to, I would listen.

I am bad at keeping secrets,
so the roosters tell me nothing.

Maybe it's not a song at all, maybe they crow with
morning stress. Maybe they dreamed
about their mothers. Do all roosters
believe their mothers do not love them?
Is this the way we've organized their lives
on farms? Is it possible for animals to be happy on farms?
What if all the roosters need more love
than they're getting?

What if I'm talking about myself, saying
sideways what I don't want to say explicitly:
I'm not getting enough love. This whole scene
doesn't love me enough. I mean, love
in the form of safety. I don't want to be
surrounded by police. This is a school.

Is it possible to be happy in a school?
I don't want to hide under a desk.
I don't want to wake up angry.
I don't want to bark at dogs.
Roosters crow, I get it now:
It's an alarm.

Notes

Several of these poems are for Mike Oliver (1981-2002), with love.

“Knoxville” is for Heather Heyer, murdered by a white supremacist mob in Charlottesville, Virginia in 2017.

“Kindle No Fires” won the 2018 Liam Rector Poetry Prize, judged by Judith Vollmer.

“Bears Protect the Town,” “El Esqueleto Humano,” “Grass, Leaves, Salt, Mud,” and “Orozco and the Disco Queen,” were awarded Honorable Mention in The Elizabeth Sloan Tyler Memorial Award.

“Arms and Legs” was inspired by the series of murals entitled “The Epic of American Civilization” by José Clemente Orozco, in the basement of Baker Library at Dartmouth College.

“The Lady with the Unicorn” was inspired by *La Dame à la licorne*, a series of tapestries in the Musée de Cluny in Paris.

“The Emperor of Ice-Cream” takes its title from Wallace Stevens.

“Skunk Hour” takes its title from Robert Lowell.

“How Abuelo Died” borrows parts of lyrics from the song “Stand by Me” written by Ben E. King, Jerry Leiber, and Mike Stoller.

“First the Fan” owes a debt of gratitude to Bob Dylan.

“Empathy Cut with Fentanyl” borrows a line from John Lennon and Paul McCartney.

“The Spider Called Maman” draws inspiration from the Louise Bourgeois sculpture “Maman” and also from her “Crouching Spider” which was on display at Dartmouth College during the 2012-13 academic year.

Acknowledgments

Many of the poems in this book have been previously published in literary magazines and anthologies, in print and online, often in a slightly different form. Heartfelt thanks to the editors and staff who make these publications possible:

Bloodroot Literary Magazine: "Artifacts";
The Common: "I See You, Gilet Jaunes";
The End of the World: "Half the Bitches in this Place Were Hanged for Treason";
Lunation: A Good Fat Anthology (Senile Monk Press, 2019): "Do Not Be Afraid";
no tokens: "The Encrypted Latina";
Poetry Crush: "No One On This Road But Us and the Night";
The Puritan: "Chango";
The Rumpus: "You Will Know Us by Our Song";
The Southampton Review: "Sweet Sixteen," "Participatory Architecture," "Empathy Cut with Fentanyl";
The Stonefence Review: "Seeing Each Other," "Hungerstrike";
The Waiting Room Reader II (Fort Lee: Cavankerry Press/UPNE, 2013): "First the Fan";
The Woven Tale Press: "Grass, Leaves, Salt, Mud," "Orozco and the Disco Queen," "Bears Protect the Town," "El Esqueleto Humano."

Cleopatra Mathis and Cynthia Huntington guided me through the rough waters of my undergraduate years, reading countless drafts of poems and encouraging me in spite of my own self-doubt. If it weren't for them, I would have given up. Lucille Clifton's guidance at that early stage was also invaluable. The Frost Place in Franconia, New Hampshire provided me with a fellowship at a very early stage in my career. It was necessary and I am grateful. Thank you, J. Hope Stein, for the extreme kindness you showed me when we first met at The Frost Place and for the following two decades of friendship. Your support is everything. Thank you, Don Pease, for hiring me to teach poetry workshops to graduate students at

Dartmouth. I hope I never let you down. Thank you, Gary Lenhart, for passing the torch to me. Thank you, Vievee Francis and Matthew Olzmann, it is an honor and a joy to be in literary community with you. Thank you to Shari Altman and Rebecca Siegel, my Literary North stars. Some of the more recent work in this book was inspired by wonderful workshops I took with Katherine Gibbel, Michael Metivier, and Laura Davies Foley at the Howe Library in Hanover, New Hampshire. Thank you, dear poets, and thank you to the excellent staff at the Howe, especially Jared Jenisch and Megan Coleman. You make the magic happen.

Heartfelt love to my writing group; Flynn Berry, Katie Crouch, Angelica del Campo, Dustin Schell, and Allie Levy. Thank you to my Left Bank family, especially Nancy Cressman and Hazel-Dawn Dumpert. Thank you to my students whose love for poetry continually refreshes my own love for poetry, especially Amanda Skinner, Meghan Kelleher, Erin Bennett, Chennelle Channer, Chelsee Niebergall, Casey Carpenter, Davey Ozahowski, TJ Riley, and James Washington.

At the Bennington Writing Seminars I had the opportunity to workshop and grow many of these poems with April Bernard, Major Jackson, Ed Ochester, and Carmen Giménez. They gave me the tools. An extra deep and abiding thank you to Mark Wunderlich who is both friend and mentor. Special thanks to Craig Morgan Teicher and Monica Farrell for having me in their workshop when I returned to Bennington as a fellow. Where would I be without Megan Galbraith? Where would any of us be? Cathy Gee Graney, my birthday twin, you are the real deal.

Thank you so much, Aracelis Girmay. Your work strikes sparks and your kindness is unparalleled. To Peter Conners, Justine Alfano, Amy Betti, Zoe LaValle, Leah Rosenman, Sandy Knight, and Isabella Madeira at BOA Editions, it is an honor to work with you. Thank you for all the time and energy you have put into this book. It means the world.

Thank you to the Stoner Women (née Stoner Chicks). You know who you are. I love you. Thank you, Rocky Point, for taking me in and making me feel like a long-lost cousin. Marisa Berwald, thank you for being my forever friend. Love to Devika Mynahan and her warm, wonderful family. To Jess Lyons, Eric Sebert and Kevin Miller, part of me will always live in Paradise Gardens with you.

Poems in this book often depict my family. Thank you, Irene; thank you, Marc & Maira & Remedios; thank you, Mario & Magda. I am deeply grateful for your unconditional love and support. Most importantly, thank you Jed Dobson, my lighthouse. Without you this ship would have wrecked a long time ago. This book is for you.

About the Author

Rena J. Mosteirin teaches creative writing workshops at Dartmouth College and owns Left Bank Books, a used bookstore in Hanover, New Hampshire. She is the author of *Experiment 116* (Counterpath Press, 2021) and co-author, with James E. Dobson, of *Moonbit* (punctum books, 2019) and *Perceptron* (punctum books, 2025). Her novella *Nick Trail's Thumb* (Kore Press, 2008) won the Kore Press Short Fiction Award, judged by Lydia Davis. Her work has been published in *The Common*, *The Rumpus*, *New York Magazine*, *New England Review*, *The Southampton Review*, *no tokens*, *The Puritan*, and elsewhere in print and online. Mosteirin is an editor at *Bloodroot Literary Magazine* and holds an MFA from the Bennington Writing Seminars.

BOA Editions, Ltd. American Poets Continuum Series

No. 1 *The Fuhrer Bunker: A Cycle of Poems in Progress*
W. D. Snodgrass

No. 2 *She*
M. L. Rosenthal

No. 3 *Living With Distance*
Ralph J. Mills, Jr.

No. 4 *Not Just Any Death*
Michael Waters

No. 5 *That Was Then: New and Selected Poems*
Isabella Gardner

No. 6 *Things That Happen Where There Aren't Any People*
William Stafford

No. 7 *The Bridge of Change: Poems 1974–1980*
John Logan

No. 8 *Signatures*
Joseph Stroud

No. 9 *People Live Here: Selected Poems 1949–1983*
Louis Simpson

No. 10 *Yin*
Carolyn Kizer

No. 11 *Duhamel: Ideas of Order in Little Canada*
Bill Tremblay

No. 12 *Seeing It Was So*
Anthony Piccione

No. 13 *Hyam Plutzik: The Collected Poems*

No. 14 *Good Woman: Poems and a Memoir 1969–1980*
Lucille Clifton

No. 15 *Next: New Poems*
Lucille Clifton

No. 16 *Roxa: Voices of the Culver Family*
William B. Patrick

No. 17 *John Logan: The Collected Poems*

No. 18 *Isabella Gardner: The Collected Poems*

No. 19 *The Sunken Lightship*
Peter Makuck

No. 20 *The City in Which I Love You*
Li-Young Lee

No. 21 *Quilting: Poems 1987–1990*
Lucille Clifton

No. 22 *John Logan: The Collected Fiction*

No. 23 *Shenandoah and Other Verse Plays*
Delmore Schwartz

No. 24 *Nobody Lives on Arthur Godfrey Boulevard*
Gerald Costanzo

No. 25 *The Book of Names: New and Selected Poems*
Barton Sutter

No. 26 *Each in His Season*
W. D. Snodgrass

No. 27 *Wordworks: Poems Selected and New*
Richard Kostelanetz

No. 28 *What We Carry*
Dorianne Laux

No. 29 *Red Suitcase*
Naomi Shihab Nye

No. 30 *Song*
Brigit Pegeen Kelly

No. 31 *The Fuehrer Bunker: The Complete Cycle*
W. D. Snodgrass

No. 32 *For the Kingdom*
Anthony Piccione

No. 33 *The Quicken Tree*
Bill Knott

No. 34 *These Upraised Hands*
William B. Patrick

No. 35 *Crazy Horse in Stillness*
William Heyen

No. 36 *Quick, Now, Always*
Mark Irwin

No. 37 *I Have Tasted the Apple*
Mary Crow

No. 38 *The Terrible Stories*
Lucille Clifton

No. 39 *The Heat of Arrivals*
Ray Gonzalez

No. 40 *Jimmy & Rita*
Kim Addonizio

No. 41 *Green Ash, Red Maple, Black Gum*
Michael Waters

No. 42 *Against Distance*
Peter Makuck

No. 43 *The Night Path*
Laurie Kutchins

No. 44 *Radiography*
Bruce Bond

No. 45 *At My Ease: Uncollected Poems of the Fifties and Sixties*
David Ignatow

No. 46 *Trillium*
Richard Foerster

No. 47 *Fuel*
Naomi Shihab Nye

No. 48 *Gratitude*
Sam Hamill

No. 49 *Diana, Charles, & the Queen*
William Heyen

No. 50 *Plus Shipping*
Bob Hicok

No. 51 *Cabato Sentora*
Ray Gonzalez

No. 52 *We Didn't Come Here for This*
William B. Patrick

No. 53 *The Vandals*
Alan Michael Parker

No. 54 *To Get Here*
Wendy Mnookin

No. 55 *Living Is What I Wanted: Last Poems*
David Ignatow

No. 56 *Dusty Angel*
Michael Blumenthal

No. 57 *The Tiger Iris*
Joan Swift

No. 58 *White City*
Mark Irwin

No. 59 *Laugh at the End of the World: Collected Comic Poems 1969–1999*
Bill Knott

No. 60 *Blessing the Boats: New and Selected Poems: 1988–2000*
Lucille Clifton

No. 61 *Tell Me*
Kim Addonizio

No. 62 *Smoke*
Dorianne Laux

No. 63 *Parthenopi: New and Selected Poems*
Michael Waters

No. 64 *Rancho Notorious*
Richard Garcia

No. 65 *Jam*
Joe-Anne McLaughlin

No. 66 *A. Poulin, Jr. Selected Poems*
Edited, with an Introduction by Michael Waters

No. 67 *Small Gods of Grief*
Laure-Anne Bosselaar

No. 68 *Book of My Nights*
Li-Young Lee

No. 69 *Tulip Farms and Leper Colonies*
Charles Harper Webb

No. 70 *Double Going*
Richard Foerster

No. 71 *What He Took*
Wendy Mnookin

No. 72 *The Hawk Temple at Tierra Grande*
Ray Gonzalez

No. 73 *Mules of Love*
Ellen Bass

No. 74 *The Guests at the Gate*
Anthony Piccione

No. 75 *Dumb Luck*
Sam Hamill

No. 76 *Love Song with Motor Vehicles*
Alan Michael Parker

No. 77 *Life Watch*
Willis Barnstone

No. 78 *The Owner of the House: New Collected Poems 1940–2001*
Louis Simpson

No. 79 *Is*
Wayne Dodd

No. 80 *Late*
Cecilia Woloch

No. 81 *Precipitates*
Debra Kang Dean

No. 82 *The Orchard*
Brigit Pegeen Kelly

No. 83 *Bright Hunger*
Mark Irwin

No. 84 *Desire Lines: New and Selected Poems*
Lola Haskins

No. 85 *Curious Conduct*
Jeanne Marie Beaumont

No. 86 *Mercy*
Lucille Clifton

No. 87 *Model Homes*
Wayne Koestenbaum

No. 88 *Farewell to the Starlight in Whiskey*
Barton Sutter

No. 89 *Angels for the Burning*
David Mura

No. 90 *The Rooster's Wife*
Russell Edson

No. 91 *American Children*
Jim Simmerman

No. 92 *Postcards from the Interior*
Wyn Cooper

No. 93 *You & Yours*
Naomi Shihab Nye

No. 94 *Consideration of the Guitar: New and Selected Poems 1986–2005*
Ray Gonzalez

No. 95 *Off-Season in the Promised Land*
Peter Makuck

No. 96 *The Hoopoe's Crown*
Jacqueline Osherow

No. 97 *Not for Specialists: New and Selected Poems*
W. D. Snodgrass

No. 98 *Splendor*
Steve Kronen

No. 99 *Woman Crossing a Field*
Deena Linett

No. 100 *The Burning of Troy*
Richard Foerster

No. 101 *Darling Vulgarity*
Michael Waters

No. 102 *The Persistence of Objects*
Richard Garcia

No. 103 *Slope of the Child Everlasting*
Laurie Kutchins

No. 104 *Broken Hallelujahs*
Sean Thomas Dougherty

No. 105 *Peeping Tom's Cabin: Comic Verse 1928–2008*
X. J. Kennedy

No. 106 *Disclamor*
G.C. Waldrep

No. 107 *Encouragement for a Man Falling to His Death*
Christopher Kennedy

No. 108 *Sleeping with Houdini*
Nin Andrews

No. 109 *Nomina*
Karen Volkman

No. 110 *The Fortieth Day*
Kazim Ali

No. 111 *Elephants & Butterflies*
Alan Michael Parker

No. 112 *Voices*
Lucille Clifton

No. 113 *The Moon Makes Its Own Plea*
Wendy Mnookin

No. 114 *The Heaven-Sent Leaf*
Katy Lederer

No. 115 *Struggling Times*
Louis Simpson

No. 116 *And*
Michael Blumenthal

No. 117 *Carpathia*
Cecilia Woloch

No. 118 *Seasons of Lotus, Seasons of Bone*
Matthew Shenoda

No. 119 *Sharp Stars*
Sharon Bryan

No. 120 *Cool Auditor*
Ray Gonzalez

No. 121 *Long Lens: New and Selected Poems*
Peter Makuck

No. 122 *Chaos Is the New Calm*
Wyn Cooper

No. 123 *Diwata*
Barbara Jane Reyes

No. 124 *Burning of the Three Fires*
Jeanne Marie Beaumont

No. 125 *Sasha Sings the Laundry on the Line*
Sean Thomas Dougherty

No. 126 *Your Father on the Train of Ghosts*
G.C. Waldrep and John Gallaher

No. 127 *Ennui Prophet*
Christopher Kennedy

No. 128 *Transfer*
Naomi Shihab Nye

No. 129 *Gospel Night*
Michael Waters

No. 130 *The Hands of Strangers: Poems from the Nursing Home*
Janice N. Harrington

No. 131 *Kingdom Animalia*
Aracelis Girmay

No. 132 *True Faith*
Ira Sadoff

No. 133 *The Reindeer Camps and Other Poems*
Barton Sutter

No. 134 *The Collected Poems of Lucille Clifton: 1965–2010*

No. 135 *To Keep Love Blurry*
Craig Morgan Teicher

No. 136 *Theophobia*
Bruce Beasley

No. 137 *Refuge*
Adrie Kusserow

No. 138 *The Book of Goodbyes*
Jillian Weise

No. 139 *Birth Marks*
Jim Daniels

No. 140 *No Need of Sympathy*
Fleda Brown

No. 141 *There's a Box in the Garage You Can Beat with a Stick*
Michael Teig

No. 142 *The Keys to the Jail*
Keetje Kuipers

No. 143 *All You Ask for Is Longing: New and Selected Poems 1994–2014*
Sean Thomas Dougherty

No. 144 *Copia*
Erika Meitner

No. 145 *The Chair: Prose Poems*
Richard Garcia

No. 146 *In a Landscape*
John Gallaher

No. 147 *Fanny Says*
Nickole Brown

No. 148 *Why God Is a Woman*
Nin Andrews

No. 149 *Testament*
G.C. Waldrep

No. 150 *I'm No Longer Troubled by the Extravagance*
Rick Bursky

No. 151 *Antidote for Night*
Marsha de la O

No. 152 *Beautiful Wall*
Ray Gonzalez

No. 153 *the black maria*
Aracelis Girmay

No. 154 *Celestial Joyride*
Michael Waters

No. 155 *Whereso*
Karen Volkman

No. 156 *The Day's Last Light Reddens the Leaves of the Copper Beech*
Stephen Dobyns

No. 157 *The End of Pink*
Kathryn Nuernberger

No. 158 *Mandatory Evacuation*
Peter Makuck

No. 159 *Primitive: The Art and Life of Horace H. Pippin*
Janice N. Harrington

No. 160 *The Trembling Answers*
Craig Morgan Teicher

No. 161 *Bye-Bye Land*
Christian Barter

No. 162 *Sky Country*
Christine Kitano

No. 163 *All Soul Parts Returned*
Bruce Beasley

No. 164 *The Smoke of Horses*
Charles Rafferty

No. 165 *The Second O of Sorrow*
Sean Thomas Dougherty

No. 166 *Holy Moly Carry Me*
Erika Meitner

No. 167 *Clues from the Animal Kingdom*
Christopher Kennedy

No. 168 *Dresses from the Old Country*
Laura Read

No. 169 *In Country*
Hugh Martin

No. 170 *The Tiny Journalist*
Naomi Shihab Nye

No. 171 *All Its Charms*
Keetje Kuipers

No. 172 *Night Angler*
Geffrey Davis

No. 173 *The Human Half*
Deborah Brown

No. 174 *Cyborg Detective*
Jillian Weise

No. 175 *On the Shores of Welcome Home*
Bruce Weigl

No. 176 *Rue*
Kathryn Nuernberger

No. 177 *Let's Become a Ghost Story*
Rick Bursky

No. 178 *Year of the Dog*
Deborah Paredez

No. 179 *Brand New Spacesuit*
John Gallaher

No. 180 *How to Carry Water: Selected Poems of Lucille Clifton*
Edited, with an Introduction by Aracelis Girmay

No. 181 *Caw*
Michael Waters

No. 182 *Letters to a Young Brown Girl*
Barbara Jane Reyes

No. 183 *Mother Country*
Elana Bell

No. 184 *Welcome to Sonnetville, New Jersey*
Craig Morgan Teicher

No. 185 *I Am Not Trying to Hide My Hungers from the World*
Kendra DeColo

No. 186 *The Naomi Letters*
Rachel Mennies

No. 187 *Tenderness*
Derrick Austin

No. 188 *Ceive*
B.K. Fischer

No. 189 *Diamonds*
Camille Guthrie

No. 190 *A Cluster of Noisy Planets*
Charles Rafferty

No. 191 *Useful Junk*
Erika Meitner

No. 192 *Field Notes from the Flood Zone*
Heather Sellers

No. 193 *A Season in Hell with Rimbaud*
Dustin Pearson

No. 194 *Your Emergency Contact Has Experienced an Emergency*
Chen Chen

No. 195 *A Tinderbox in Three Acts*
Cynthia Dewi Oka

No. 196 *Little Mr. Prose Poem: Selected Poems of Russell Edson*
Edited by Craig Morgan Teicher

No. 197 *The Dug-Up Gun Museum*
Matt Donovan

No. 198 *Four in Hand*
Alicia Mountain

No. 199 *Buffalo Girl*
Jessica Q. Stark

No. 200 *Nomenclatures of Invisibility*
Mahtem Shiferraw

No. 201 *Flare, Corona*
Jeannine Hall Gailey

No. 202 *Death Prefers the Minor Keys*
Sean Thomas Dougherty

No. 203 *Desire Museum*
Danielle Deulen

No. 204 *Transitory*
Subhaga Crystal Bacon

No. 205 *Every Hard Sweetness*
Sheila Carter-Jones

No. 206 *Blue on a Blue Palette*
Lynne Thompson

No. 207 *One Wild Word Away*
Geffrey Davis

No. 208 *The Strange God Who Makes Us*
Christopher Kennedy

No. 209 *Our Splendid Failure to Do the Impossible*
Rebecca Lindenberg

No. 210 *Yard Show*
Janice N. Harrington

No. 211 *The Last Song of the World*
Joseph Fasano

No. 212 *Lonely Women Make Good Lovers*
Keetje Kuipers

No. 213 *jump the gun*
Jennie Malboeuf

No. 214 *Apostle of Desire*
Bruce Weigl

No. 215 *GREEN OF ALL HEADS*
Aracelis Girmay

No. 216 *Pluck*
Adam Hughes

No. 217 *Disaster Tourism*
Rena J. Mosteirin

Colophon

BOA Editions, Ltd., a nonprofit publisher of poetry and other literary works, fosters readership and appreciation of contemporary literature. By identifying, cultivating, and publishing both new and established poets and selecting authors of unique literary talent, BOA brings high-quality literature to the public. Support for this effort comes from the sale of its publications, grant funding, and private donations.

The publication of this book is made possible, in part, by the special support of the following individuals:

Anonymous (x2)
Ralph Black & Susan Murphy
Angela Bonazinga & Catherine Lewis
Bernadette Catalana
Gwen Conners, *in memory of June Baker*
Chris Dahl, *in honor of Chuck Hertrick*
Jonathan Everitt
Bonnie Garner
James Hale
Grant Holcomb
Nora A. Jones
Joe & Dale Klein
Barbara Lovenheim, *in memory of John Lovenheim*
Joe McElveney
John & Judy Messenger
Dorrie Parini
Boo Poulin, *in memory of A. Poulin Jr.*
Michael Quattrone
Deborah Ronnen
John H. Schultz
William Waddell & Linda Rubel